Original title:
Passion in Action

Copyright © 2024 Swan Charm
All rights reserved.

Editor: Jessica Elisabeth Luik
Author: Swan Charm
ISBN HARDBACK: 978-9916-86-248-3
ISBN PAPERBACK: 978-9916-86-249-0

Torrential Spirits

In the hush of dusk, the spirits wake,
Whispers dance on the misty lake.
Shadows stretch, then softly break,
Dreams unfold with every quake.

Rain pours down, a silver veil,
Embrace the night, so dark and frail.
Echoes of the past, they sail,
Woven tales in stormy gale.

Ghostly lights in tempests shine,
Guiding hearts through the divine.
Through the storm, the stars align,
Binding fates, in sacred sign.

Winds will howl and tears may stream,
Fjord of night where phantoms dream.
Boundless realms where echoes gleam,
Life and death, a twilight scheme.

We'll endure the tempests' might,
In torrential spirits' flight.
Love and sorrow intertwine,
Eternal dance, in moonlit pine.

Searing Echoes

Whispers burnt in twilight's hue,
A dance of shadows, old and new.
In the silence, rhythms play,
Searing echoes, night and day.

Feathered leaves of autumn's sway,
Murmurs of a distant fray.
Timeless moments etched in stone,
Searing echoes, all alone.

Eyes that gaze into the night,
Seeking truths beyond the light.
Every heartbeat quietly suspires,
Searing echoes, hidden fires.

Epic Fires

From the depths of ancient lore,
Rise the flames forevermore.
Storytellers weave and spin,
Epic fires deep within.

Heroes tread through mortal fears,
Carving paths of countless years.
Roaring flames that dare to try,
Epic fires reach the sky.

Legends cast in fiery glow,
Tales of triumph, ebb and flow.
Burning hearts, their minds inspire,
Epic fires, souls' desire.

Dynamic Symphony

Notes that dance beneath the stars,
Melodies that heal our scars.
In the wind, a voice so free,
Dynamic symphony, you and me.

Strings that whisper through the night,
Guiding dreams with pure delight.
Every sound, a world apart,
Dynamic symphony, beating heart.

Rhythms pulse in earnest chase,
Time and space, a boundless grace.
Music's touch, so wild, so free,
Dynamic symphony, destiny.

Unchained Zeal

A spirit born of endless fire,
Wings that span a heart's desire.
Boundaries break and shadows yield,
Unchained zeal in open field.

Eyes like comets, fierce and bright,
Through the dark, they share their light.
No tethered dreams, no silent plea,
Unchained zeal, eternally.

Mountains bow and rivers part,
Guided by a fervent heart.
In the quest, the truth revealed,
Unchained zeal, forever steeled.

Luminous Drive

In the quiet dawn, a spark ignites
Whispered dreams take flight, unseen.
Through mist and fog, the pathway bends,
Guided by a light serene.

Ambitions glow in the morning's hue,
A journey vast, both near and wide.
With every step, a sunburst shines,
Against the shadows, bright inside.

Hope alight in the crisp fresh dew,
Footprints mapping endless strives.
Buoyant heart in the radiant morn,
This is the path of luminous drives.

Ebullient Spirit

In the heart's resplendent core,
Dance the dreams untamed, unsheathed.
Burgeoning breaths of life untold,
Ebullient spirit, freely breathed.

O'er mountains high and valleys low,
Roars the laughter of pure delight.
Cresting waves of boundless joy,
In sacred days and endless night.

Every step a revelry,
In cosmic twine, by fate's own guise.
Revel in this wild embrace,
For in spirit, we truly rise.

Dynamic Obsession

In the spiral dance of fate,
Passion whirls in fervent chase.
Eyes alight with burning fire,
Tides of destinies interlace.

Echoed heartbeats, thunderous drum,
Chase the dreams relentlessly.
Winds of change beneath our wings,
Soar through skies unstintingly.

Force and fervor, drive unbound,
Each moment seized in fleeting trust.
A life lived in dynamic pull,
With every breath, a fervid gust.

Vigorous Quest

Beneath the skies of endless scope,
A call to arms, a knightly vow.
Seek the truth within the storm,
Hold the courage on your brow.

Through brambles thick and rivers wide,
Steady heart, unyielding zest.
In the trials, find your might,
For life's a quest, a vigorous test.

Beyond the hills, the vales unseen,
In shadows deep and heights so blessed.
With every stride, with all your strength,
Embrace the quest, give it your best.

Dreams in Overdrive

Beneath the moon, the stars align,
Whispers of dreams, in a dance so fine.
Through twilight's veil, ambitions thrive,
Echoes of hope, dreams in overdrive.

Heartbeats meld with the night's rhythm,
Painting paths where futures glisten.
In silent symphony, dreams arrive,
Carried on wings, dreams in overdrive.

Night's embrace, a canvas wide,
Where fantasies and truths collide.
Within each twinkle, tales contrive,
Boundless and free, dreams in overdrive.

Soul's Blaze

In the shadow, a light we chase,
A flicker born from a soul's embrace.
Amidst the dark, a radiant phase,
Eternal flame, this soul's blaze.

Courage shines where fears once lied,
Strength awakens with every stride.
Through storm and storm, through wild maze,
Unyielding light, the soul's blaze.

From ashes cold, a phoenix soars,
Burning bright, embracing more.
Against the night, in fervent praise,
Undying fire, the soul's blaze.

Unstoppable Force

Tides may rise and mountains tall,
Yet forward we press, through it all.
With every step, we set the course,
Unleashed within, an unstoppable force.

Valleys deep and canyons wide,
Cannot deter what burns inside.
Through trials faced, we'll never pause,
Relentless drive, an unstoppable force.

Upward bound, through skies unknown,
Together we, our strength has grown.
In unity, we'll chart our source,
Bound by heart, an unstoppable force.

Horizon Chase

Beneath a sky of endless hues,
On dreams we sail, with morning's clues.
Across the vast and open space,
We journey forth, in a horizon chase.

Mountains echo tales of old,
Rivers whisper secrets untold.
Through dawn's embrace, at nature's pace,
Our spirits soar, in a horizon chase.

Unknown realms and distant shores,
We seek the light, forever more.
In serendipity's tender grace,
We find our way, in a horizon chase.

Perpetual Blaze

In twilight's gentle, fleeting haze,
A fire starts its fervent chase.
With whispered sparks that softly graze,
It builds a grand, perpetual blaze.

Through verdant fields and rugged ways,
It spreads its warmth, its bright bouquets.
In every heart, it finds a place,
A constant glow in life's embrace.

It dances high, it weaves, it sways,
Through nights and days, it never stays.
In every soul, its zeal displays,
A testament to endless days.

Ardent Stride

With every dawn, an ardent stride,
A journey through the great divide.
The mountains steep, the valleys wide,
Our hopes and dreams, we won't deride.

The winds of change, they swiftly glide,
Through tangled paths, we must decide.
In every heart, a flame inside,
To face the storm, our fears will bide.

With courage as our trusted guide,
Across the seas, the stars will slide.
In unity, we all confide,
To reach the peak, our spirits tied.

Effervescent Goals

In starlit dreams and whispered souls,
Lie secrets of effervescent goals.
They shimmer bright as twilight scrolls,
Through endless skies, as night unfolds.

With every step, a vision molds,
On paths of gold, through life it strolls.
In challenges, our strength consoles,
Our will and might, the heart extols.

Through tempest winds and ceaseless tolls,
We chase the light, where future rolls.
In every pulse, ambition scrolls,
To heights unknown, our spirit bolts.

Searing Momentum

As dawn's first light begins to crest,
We set our hopes on life's great quest.
In every heart, a burning zest,
A searing momentum, we're blessed.

Through trials steep, we give our best,
In every challenge, stand the test.
With passion's fire, we feel possessed,
To soar above, and never rest.

With dreams alive, our souls attest,
To futures bright, the sky's caressed.
In unity, we feel compressed,
A searing force, we manifest.

Blissful Persistence

In gardens wet with morning dew,
We find the path to wander through,
With every step the heart renews,
A journey crafted always true.

The sun, it rises, bold and bright,
Casting shadows, soft as night,
Through trials faced with gentle might,
We keep the flame of hope alight.

Our dreams may waver, some may bend,
Yet spirits climb, not seek an end,
In every challenge, friend to friend,
We promise to the stars, ascend.

The world, a canvas yet to paint,
With vivid hues, we shan't be faint,
For through persistence, life's a saint,
In moments grand, or those so quaint.

With passion tethered to our core,
We venture boldly, evermore,
To see, to seek, what lies in store,
In blissful persistence, we soar.

Torrid Climb

Beneath the sun, the fervor grows,
A path unknown, yet onward shows,
With grit and sweat, our spirit knows,
The strength that in our being flows.

Cliffs of doubt and peaks of strife,
Mark the journey, shape the life,
With every climb and careful knife,
We carve our tale in bold relief.

The heat, it burns, yet heart persists,
In every fall, a clenched fist,
We rise with dawn's unfading twist,
In torrid climb, by dreams we're kissed.

With every step, a lesson learned,
Through fires bright, our souls discerned,
For heights we seek are dearly earned,
By flames within that ever burned.

The summit calls, where skies embrace,
With weary limbs, we find our place,
A torrid climb, a noble chase,
In every trial, there's boundless grace.

Vivacious Dreams

In moonlit fields where shadows play,
Our vivid dreams do softly sway,
They beckon us to cast away,
The fears that haunt the light of day.

With whispers soft, and colors bright,
They dance upon the edge of night,
Inviting hearts to take delight,
In moments woven pure and light.

The stars above in silent scheme,
Reflect the magic of our dream,
An endless thread, a vibrant theme,
In night's embrace, they softly gleam.

With eyes closed tight, yet vision clear,
We chase the dreams, both far and near,
Each step is bold, devoid of fear,
In every breath, their call we hear.

So let us weave with tender seam,
A tapestry of hope's esteem,
To live, to love, to boldly deem,
Our path be laced with vivacious dream.

Turbulent Joy

In winds that howl, in storms that rage,
We find the pulse upon life's stage,
Amidst the chaos, we engage,
In turbulent joy, we set the gauge.

The laughter bursts in tempest's core,
A wild ride we can't ignore,
Through twists and turns, we still implore,
To feel the thrill, to seek out more.

Each moment sharp, like broken glass,
Yet joy does rise, it does amass,
In midst of conflict, bold and brash,
We find the calm within the clash.

The heart, it beats with fervent fire,
A symphony of high desire,
In clouds of gray, we do aspire,
To touch the sparks, to rise up higher.

With every storm, there's stark delight,
In chaos, dreams take winged flight,
Through turbulent joy, we find our sight,
In restless waves, we find the light.

Sparkling Marathon

In the twilight, paths unfold,
Steps like echoes, stories told.
Through the night, our spirits fly,
Dreams ignited, touch the sky.

Every heartbeat, sprints anew,
Chasing stars, we're breaking through.
Miles ahead, the journey gleams,
Endless roads, endless dreams.

Boundless skies beneath our feet,
Rhythms of our pulse, so sweet.
To the horizon, shadows flee,
In this dance, we run free.

Whispers of the dawn embrace,
Moments hush, in silent grace.
Tides of hope, tides of light,
Guide us through this endless night.

Eternal chase, in twilight's sheen,
Bound by hope, through valleys green.
In every stride, a bright new dawn,
This sparkling marathon.

Undying Blaze

Beneath the stars, the embers grow,
Silent whispers, soft and slow.
In the heart, a fire bright,
Igniting depths of darkest night.

Through the storm, the spirit flares,
Rising high, on winds and prayers.
Flames of passion, never cease,
In their warmth, we find our peace.

Veins of courage, blood of dreams,
Flowing wild, in endless streams.
Ashes bloom, from fiery days,
In the glow of undying blaze.

Every spark, a story told,
In the embers, tales unfold.
Against the cold, we fiercely stand,
Fire within, guides our hand.

Bound by flames, our souls reborn,
In the hearth, where light is sworn.
Forever bright, in darkest maze,
Shines the light, of undying blaze.

Resolute Euphoria

Through the mists, a light appears,
Chasing skies and vanquished fears.
In the heart, a song resounds,
Resolute euphoria found.

Echoes of the past erased,
With each step, new dreams embraced.
Hope like beams, it lifts the soul,
Guiding onwards, making whole.

Hearts entwined, we face the tide,
In this journey, side by side.
Bound by strength, and love so sure,
In euphoria, we endure.

Timeless dance beneath the stars,
Moments held in memory jars.
Through the night, our spirits soar,
Higher dreams forevermore.

Boundless joy, in every breath,
In the face of life and death.
In the light, we rise and shine,
Resolute, this joy is mine.

Explosive Goals

Dreams like rockets, taking flight,
Blazing trails through darkest night.
Hopes ignited, visions clear,
Explosive goals, we persevere.

Through the struggles, strength is found,
In our veins, ambition's sound.
Every heartbeat, a new quest,
Striving always, for our best.

In the face of doubt, we rise,
Stars reflected in our eyes.
With each step, our spirits soar,
Breaking limits, seeking more.

Passion fuels this burning drive,
In our hearts, we're so alive.
Leap of faith, and courage bold,
Pursuing dreams, untold gold.

Bound by vision, clear and bright,
Guided by this inner light.
In each effort, we console,
Reaching out for explosive goals.

Electric Whispers

In a night of soundless dreams,
Electric whispers weave the seams,
Glimmers pulse through starlit air,
Silent echoes everywhere.

Lightning dances in the sky,
Neon whispers rushing by,
A murmured secret, faint and clear,
Electric whispers, drawing near.

Veils of darkness softly part,
Currents intertwine the heart,
Whispers hush and shadows blend,
Electric whispers, never end.

Inferno of the Soul

Tempered fire, fierce and bright,
Raging through the endless night,
Burning fiercely, untamed force,
Inferno of the soul, of course.

In the blaze, our secrets lie,
Truths revealed and shadows die,
Cinders dance on flames below,
Inferno of the soul aglow.

Ashes fall like whispered dreams,
Life reformed by ardent beams,
Flames consume and make us whole,
Inferno of the burning soul.

Canvas of Yearning

On a canvas soft and bare,
Brushstrokes lit with tender care,
Colors blend where dreams take flight,
Canvas of yearning, pure and bright.

Longing hues and shades profound,
In each stroke, our hopes are bound,
Layers deep where hearts do rest,
Canvas yearns for love confessed.

Every inch a tale untold,
Crimson passion, deep and bold,
Yearning paints an endless sea,
Canvas of our destiny.

Driven by Flame

Through the dark, we forge our way,
Driven by the flame that stays,
Passion's fire within our core,
Flame that pushes, evermore.

In the heat, our spirits rise,
Burning truth within our eyes,
Driven by the calls of fate,
Flame that neither time nor hate.

Fires burn and embers stay,
Guiding us through night to day,
Driven by a flame so pure,
Through the blaze, our souls endure.

Luminary Efforts

Through darkened paths, a light does gleam,
A beacon in the midnight stream.
With every step, the shadows flee,
A journey marked by destiny.

Unseen hands guide with gentle care,
Through trials met with strength laid bare.
In twilight's realm, resolve remains,
Forging hope from life's refrains.

The stars align in silent grace,
Mapping dreams across time's space.
In every heart, a spark ignites,
A testament to endless nights.

From dawn to dusk, in cyclical dance,
Purpose woven in circumstance.
An inner light that never fades,
Through all of life's uncertain shades.

And as the luminescence grows,
Each effort shines, and brightly shows.
A tapestry of hopes combined,
The luminary path aligned.

Steadfast Flames

In hearths of hope, the flames arise,
A testament to countless tries.
Through wind and storm, they fiercely burn,
A steady light at every turn.

Embers glow in twilight's breath,
Defying time, outlasting death.
With courage stoked by whispered gales,
Their warmth prevails, no effort fails.

A beacon through the darkest night,
In steadfast hearts, a guiding light.
The flames of hope, in constant blaze,
Illuminating unseen ways.

When shadows seek to snuff the spark,
In embers' glow, we'll leave our mark.
A legacy of living fire,
Unyielding light, our true desire.

And so each flame, unwavering strong,
Continues forth, where we belong.
In unity, our spirits claim,
The undying power of steadfast flame.

Vibrant Endeavors

In colors bold and spirits bright,
We chase our dreams through day and night.
With vibrant steps, the world we grace,
In every heart, we find our place.

A tapestry of efforts seen,
In each endeavor, dreams convene.
Through trials faced with colors high,
We paint our future in the sky.

The brush of life, in hands so true,
Creates a canvas wide and new.
With every stroke, a story told,
In vibrant hues both brave and bold.

From dawn to dusk, our spirits soar,
In every shade, our hearts implore.
To seek, to find, to not relent,
In vibrant waves, our lives are spent.

And in the end, the colors blend,
In echoes that will never end.
Our vibrant endeavors will remain,
A legacy of joy and pain.

Fierce Dynamics

In motion swift, the currents run,
A dance beneath the rising sun.
With fierce resolve, the tides we ride,
In dynamic waves, our fates reside.

Through storms we sail, with hearts full strong,
In rhythms fierce, we find our song.
Unyielding force and constant drive,
In every pulse, we thrive, alive.

With every surge, the future calls,
A journey's path through unseen halls.
In ebb and flow, our spirits rise,
Defying limits, touching skies.

In unity, we face the storm,
In fierce dynamics, true and warm.
Our energies in constant play,
Navigating night and day.

And when the final wave has passed,
In echoes fierce, our dreams will last.
For in the dance of life's expanse,
We find our strength, and take our chance.

Eclipsed Fervor

Silent whispers in the night,
Stars obscured by shadow's flight.
Lost in dreams of pure embrace,
Heartbeats echo in the space.

Moonlight fades, an ember's glow,
Passion's tide ebbs, swells below.
Underneath the twilight's veil,
Love's eclipse begins to pale.

Yearning in the darkest hour,
Touched by fate's elusive power.
Eyes that search the skies above,
Find the secrets of their love.

Whispers blend in cosmic dance,
Fate and destiny, a trance.
In the void, a truth obscured,
By fervor, hearts have been lured.

In Full Throttle

Engines roaring, hearts collide,
Speed of light, we will not hide.
Chasing dreams in open sky,
On the edge, we soar and fly.

Winds of fate, beneath each wing,
In the thrill, our souls will sing.
Gravity, a fleeting thought,
In this rush, we're never caught.

Through the curves and twists of life,
Cutting air like sharpened knife.
Boundless spirit, wild and free,
In full throttle, destiny.

Racing stars and blazing trails,
In the echoes, victory hails.
Life unfolds in rapid streams,
In full throttle, chase your dreams.

Ignition Point

Spark ignites, a flame reborn,
In the night, a star is torn.
Passions flare in fierce delight,
Fueling dreams that take to flight.

Energy from sparks unchained,
Through the dark, a hope regained.
Fires burn with fervent might,
Lighting paths through endless night.

Every heart with embers bright,
Seeks the dawn to end the fight.
Ignition point of bold desire,
Turns the dark to morning fire.

Rise from ashes, spirits soar,
Blaze a trail and search for more.
Kindle flames of dreams in plight,
Ignition, set the world alight.

Radiant Crusade

Rise and cast away the night,
In the dawn's first golden light.
March with purpose, hearts ablaze,
Guide your steps in untold ways.

Shields that glimmer, swords that gleam,
Chasing shadows, bold and keen.
On this journey, brave and bright,
Seek the truth, beyond the night.

Voices raised in anthem clear,
Echo strong so all will hear.
Radiant crusade of dreams,
Cut through lies and break the seams.

Battles fought with hearts afire,
Every soul with fierce desire.
In the glow of hope's cascade,
We press on, a radiant crusade.

Energy Unbound

In the dance of dawn's first light,
Passion's spark takes joyful flight,
Through the veins it swiftly streams,
Fueling thoughts with vibrant dreams.

Ripples push the stagnant sea,
Waves of change set spirits free,
Boundless hope in every rise,
Mirrors truths in endless skies.

Stars align in cosmic trace,
Galaxies in boundless chase,
Energy, a ceaseless call,
Forms a bridge, connects us all.

Heartbeat's echo, pulsing fire,
Forges pathways of desire,
In each breath, the cosmos found,
Life's true essence, energy unbound.

Threads unseen that bind our fate,
Weave the vastness, intricate,
We ignite, a spark profound,
In this realm, our spirits crowned.

Scorched by Goals

Driven by an inner flame,
Chasing shadows, no two same,
Through the trials, feeling bold,
Yet the fire leaves a toll.

In pursuit of dreams so grand,
Burning trails across the land,
Every victory, every loss,
Leaves a mark, a heavy cost.

Ambition's heat, a steady blaze,
Lights the path, a fiery maze,
Melts the doubts, clears the sight,
But consumes the darkened night.

Scars of effort, deeply known,
Lessons from the seeds we've sown,
In the ashes, wisdom's glow,
Growth through hardship, we bestow.

Through the inferno, souls refined,
Strength and purpose intertwined,
Goals attained, and burdens light,
Rise anew, in morning's light.

Whirlwind Embrace

In the storm, a quiet grace,
Whirlwind hearts in fast embrace,
Spirits soar on wild breeze,
Finding peace in chaos seas.

Eyes that meet in spinning swirl,
Lost in moments, time unfurl,
Hands enjoined in fervent bind,
Love explores the unconfined.

Drift through clouds, both soft and gray,
In this tempest, hearts convey,
Whispers caught in nature's cry,
Promises that never die.

Each embrace, a twilight hue,
Melds our worlds to something new,
In the whirlwind, find our place,
Unified in love's embrace.

Life's fierce winds may shift our ground,
Yet our bond stays circle-round,
Anchored heartbeats, fearless gaze,
Two as one, in whirlwind's maze.

Fiery Pursuits

With each dawn, a fervent quest,
Seek the spark within our chest,
Chase the winds, ignite the view,
Hopes are forged in passion's hue.

Mountains climb and rivers race,
Every heartbeat sets the pace,
Through the trials, through the flames,
Stoke the fires, fuel the aims.

Dreams like embers, burning bright,
Guide us through the dark of night,
Scorch the doubts, release the ties,
Rise anew where courage lies.

In the blaze, the truth we see,
Strength in tenacity,
Pursuits fierce, intentions true,
Find the fire within you.

Footsteps leave a glowing trail,
Tales of heart and will prevail,
Through the ashes, rise anew,
Fuel your dreams in fiery hues.

Surge of Emotion

In twilight's grasp, my heart does ache,
As moonlight whispers secrets vast.
Each sigh a testament to dreams,
That in the night, forever last.

The waves of feeling crash ashore,
A tempest brewing in my soul.
With every crest, my love takes flight,
To heights I scarcely can control.

Emotions surge like rivers wild,
Through valleys deep and mountains high.
In rapture's grip, I stand alone,
Yet feel the world beneath me fly.

For in this storm, a truth unveiled,
That every tear and laugh combines.
A symphony of life's embrace,
In every heart, such love enshrines.

So let the torrent carry forth,
This surge of passion, boundless sea.
For in its depths, our spirits find,
The essence of our humanity.

Radiant Quest

Upon the dawn's first gentle touch,
The world awakens, dreams unfurl.
With every step, we chase the light,
In search of truth, a pearl.

Beneath the stars, we venture far,
On paths that glow with mystic gleam.
The radiant quest, a guiding flame,
Through shadowed realms, we gleam.

With courage held within our hearts,
We face the trials, fierce and strong.
Each moment birthed from hope and grace,
A stride toward where we belong.

Through verdant fields and desert sands,
This journey whispers ancient tales.
In every stride, a story weaves,
And in our souls, it never pales.

For in the quest, our spirits rise,
To grasp the dreams we've yet to find.
With every dawn, a promise new,
The radiant light, our hearts aligned.

Kindled Paths

Beneath the autumn's crimson leaves,
A path emerges, warmly lit.
With every step, a fire ignites,
In hearts that dare to dream and git.

Kindled paths through twilight's grace,
Where stories ancient, softly blend.
Each spark a guide through time and space,
A journey knowing not an end.

With steadfast souls, we wander free,
Through forests dense and valleys wide.
The flames of hope our steadfast guide,
Through every challenge, stride by stride.

In every glance, a promise made,
That paths ignited lead us true.
The flicker of the past remains,
To light the future's vibrant hue.

So let us walk with spirits bright,
On kindled paths 'neath starlit skies.
For in each step, a beacon glows,
And with our dreams, new worlds arise.

Burning Aspirations

In the heart's core, a flame ignites,
A burning wish within the gloom.
With every breath, the blaze does grow,
Inspiring dreams to fully bloom.

Aspirations fierce, like fire,
Consume the fears that once held tight.
The embers dance, a guiding light,
Through darkest night to new daylight.

With eyes aglow, we venture far,
Through trials born of scorching heat.
Upon the winds of change we ride,
To find where purpose and passion meet.

In every heart, a spark resides,
A yearning flame that won't subside.
Through sweat and tears, it's fueled anew,
Until our hopes and dreams collide.

Burn bright, ambitions deeply held,
For in your glow, our paths are clear.
With burning aspirations shared,
We forge a future without fear.

Zeal Unleashed

In morning's golden burst,
Dreams rouse with fervent gleam.
Paths ahead are steep and curved,
Fate's tapestry, a seam.

Fears dissolve in passion's stride,
The heart beats fierce and sure.
Strengthened by the dawning tide,
Undaunted, brave, and pure.

Echoes of resolve resound,
In the fervor of pursuit.
Boundless spirit, dreams unbound,
Life's symphony acute.

With each step, the soul ignites,
Vision clear and keen.
Through trials thick and endless nights,
The spirit reigns serene.

Zeal unleashed, a wildfire bright,
Burns with endless might.
In its glow, every trial slight,
Victory in sight.

Rapture of Effort

In the labor of the soul,
Joy and sweat entwine.
Striving to the final goal,
Stars in daylight shine.

Every ounce of will we spent,
In the journey's sway.
Sacrifice becomes content,
In the work and play.

Endless skies above us call,
To the heights we dare.
Each ascent defies the fall,
Winds of hope we share.

Moments where the spirit flies,
Unseen realms in reach.
Rapture in the heart's own cries,
Victory in speech.

Effort's song, a glorious tune,
Challenging the night.
In our hands the endless boon,
Of endless courage bright.

Vigorous Ventures

Into the unknown we embark,
With fervor in our stride.
Charting paths through realms stark,
No shadow where we bide.

Mysteries beckon, horizons wide,
Adventures vast and grand.
With courage as our constant guide,
We journey hand in hand.

The pulse of life within our veins,
Vigorous and true.
Through sun and storm, through joy and pains,
Our spirits ever new.

Unyielding to the tempests roar,
We carve our destiny.
Each venture opens a new door,
To boundless realms we see.

Bound by neither time nor place,
Our hearts to dreams adhere.
In vigorous ventures, we embrace,
A future bright and clear.

Determined Flames

In the heart of darkest night,
A spark begins to glow.
Kindling hope with radiant light,
Defying winds that blow.

Fires of will, so fierce and strong,
Illuminating skies.
Through the trials, our spirits long,
For dreams that never die.

With every spark, a promise burns,
Bright as morning sun.
In our veins, a passion churns,
Until the prize is won.

Unified in common fire,
Each step—a bond of flame.
Every failure, higher climb,
None to share the blame.

Determined flames, they fuel our quest,
Enduring through the end.
With each endeavor, in our chest,
A light no storm can bend.

Heartbeat in Motion

In the quiet night, a pulse aligns,
With whispered winds through olden pines.
Stars above in silent dance,
Each beat a perfect, timed romance.

Oceans breathe with tidal song,
Waves of life where hearts belong.
Every crest and every fall,
Echoes through the darkened hall.

Footsteps echo on the ground,
Silent whispers all around.
Heartbeat steady, rhythmic grace,
Binding love in time and space.

In each moment, fluid dance,
Every heartbeat, second chance.
Life's ballet moves endlessly,
Painting dreams for us to see.

Soul to soul, the currents run,
Blood and fire, spirit spun.
Heartbeat in motion, wild and free,
Love's true measure, eternity.

Euphoric Chase

Through the meadows, wild we sprint,
Sunlight dapples, golden glint.
Breathless laughter fills the air,
Euphoria beyond compare.

Mountains rise to greet the sky,
We are stars that learn to fly.
In the wind, a sweet embrace,
Lost within this joyous chase.

Flowers kiss our fleeting feet,
Nature's song, a rhythm sweet.
Here, we dance with boundless grace,
Life a never-ending race.

Time dissolves as heartbeats race,
Lost within this sacred space.
Moments turn to endless play,
Dreams unfold in light of day.

Eyes aglow with pure delight,
Chasing dreams with all our might.
Euphoric winds through souls entwine,
In this fleeting, wild divine.

Electric Zeal

Across the sky, a lightning blaze,
Sparks ignite in radiant haze.
Heartbeats sync with thundering roar,
Electric zeal forevermore.

Neon dreams in city's heart,
Every pulse, a work of art.
Wires hum with energy,
Currents charge our legacy.

Eyes alight with vibrant hues,
Electric veins in midnight blues.
Pulse of life, a writhing stream,
Surges through this waking dream.

In the chaos, find the calm,
Power hums a quiet psalm.
Each vibration, wild and bright,
We become the living light.

Energies in endless dance,
Sparks of life in sacred trance.
Electric zeal, we intertwine,
Worlds collide, and stars align.

Dancing with Dreams

In the twilight, whispers soft,
Dreams alight and spirits loft.
Moonbeams paint a silken trail,
Dancing dreams within the veil.

Footsteps trace a phantom line,
Hopes and wishes intertwine.
Silhouettes in shadowed streams,
Waltz within our secret dreams.

Breath of night, a gentle kiss,
Worlds between, a silent bliss.
Whispers through the starlit air,
Dreams and we, a perfect pair.

Eyes shut tight, the visions spin,
Stories birthed from deep within.
Mind and heart in syncopation,
In this nightly celebration.

Waking comes with morning light,
Dreams dissolve in sun's embrace.
Yet we dance with dreams at night,
In their tender, fleeting grace.

Heatwave of Hope

The sun ascends, a golden blaze,
Across a sky in truest blue,
With fervid rays that gently graze,
And promises of mornings new.

In every beam, a tale unfolds,
Of dreams that bask in warming light,
Of courage, bright and strong, that holds,
In shadows turned to purest white.

Beneath the sun, our hearts are light,
We chase the clouds that dance and flee,
To find a hope that's burning bright,
And set our souls forever free.

Each step we take, with hope we'll stride,
Through summer's heat and autumn's chill,
For in the warmth of life we bide,
And kindle dreams that time distills.

So let the sun its fervor show,
And let the heatwaves brightly weave,
A tapestry of endless glow,
In which our hearts and hopes believe.

Fervent Journeys

Beneath the stars we start our quest,
Through valleys deep and mountains high,
With every step, we're truly blessed,
As dreams take wing and hearts imply.

In every sunrise, paths unfold,
A journey fierce yet tender too,
With courage bold and spirits bold,
We'll find the truth in morning's hue.

The winds may shift, the dark may fall,
Yet still we march with hearts aglow,
For in each night, a fervent call,
That guides us where our spirits flow.

The road is endless, wide and vast,
With tales akin to ocean's crest,
But in each heartbeat, holds the past,
And in each breath, the future's quest.

So let us walk with fervent stride,
Through tempests fierce and sunsets soft,
For in the journey's ebb and tide,
We'll find our spirits lifted aloft.

Blazing Desires

In the heart of fire, we find our spark,
A blaze that sets the soul aflight,
In passions high and moments dark,
A flame that dances in the night.

Through every trial, through every tear,
Desires blaze with endless might,
A phoenix rising, free from fear,
To touch the stars, to claim the light.

With every heartbeat, wishes roar,
A symphony of dreams untold,
In blazing hopes, we yearn for more,
As stories of the brave unfold.

For in the soul, a fire ignites,
A fervent blaze, a fiery tune,
It fuels the days, sustains the nights,
A beacon 'neath the blazing moon.

So let our hearts be wild and free,
In passions' flames and bright desires,
We'll shape a world where all can see,
The beauty in our blazing fires.

Intense Devotion

In whispers soft of love's embrace,
A bond that's forged in hearts so true,
With every look, with every trace,
A devotion that the ages knew.

In twilight's glow, in dawn's first light,
We find a love both strong and pure,
Unyielding in the darkest night,
A flame that will forever endure.

Through trials faced and battles fought,
Our hearts remain unbreaking, whole,
For in our bond, devotion's wrought,
An endless fire within our soul.

Each moment shared, each silent vow,
A tapestry of love so tight,
With every breath, we both avow,
To cherish love with all our might.

So let our hearts beat strong as one,
In fierce devotion's timeless glow,
Through every moon, through every sun,
Our love's intense, and ever so.

Incandescent Will

Beneath the stars, a fire glows,
Unyielding light, where courage grows.
Against the dark, it never fears,
Burns steadfastly through endless years.

With every trial, it turns to flame,
Each spark a testament to its name.
A beacon bright in stormy night,
Guiding souls with its fierce light.

In battles deep, it stands so tall,
Against the odds, it will not fall.
No force can dim its radiant might,
An eternal blaze in darkest night.

Whispers of hope in every ember,
Stories of strength we must remember.
An incandescent will that drives,
The essence of what means to thrive.

Infinite Tenacity

Upon the mountain's steep ascent,
Where challenges so fiercely bent,
A spirit strong, relentless stride,
With every fall, it will abide.

Through winds that howl and rains that beat,
It marches on with tireless feet.
No summit high can turn its course,
Each step a testament to force.

The path is rough, the journey long,
Yet it persists, forever strong.
Resilient heart and steady breath,
Defying fate, eschewing death.

Infinite tenacity, a timeless drive,
In every storm, it will survive.
A constant flow, unceasing blaze,
Through trials, it forever stays.

Energetic Love

In every glance, a spark ignites,
A dance of souls in tender flights.
With every touch, the cosmos spins,
Boundless energy from within.

A symphony of hearts entwined,
In fervent rhythm, love defined.
Electric pulses, passion's flow,
A vivid streak in life's tableau.

Through time and space, it rushes forth,
A boundless light of utmost worth.
Unseen threads that tie and bind,
An ever-present force, unconfined.

The essence pure of joy and care,
In energetic love, we're aware.
Of every breath, a shared delight,
Illuminating darkest night.

Zealous Expedition

Beyond the realms of known and seen,
A journey starts with fervent sheen.
With eyes afire and hearts aglow,
Toward the vast unknown we go.

Through deserts dry and oceans deep,
A quest for dreams we vow to keep.
Each step a pledge to seek and find,
New worlds and wonders intertwined.

With zealous fervor, paths we carve,
In every challenge, spirits starve.
For knowledge, growth, and distant lands,
We traverse wide with eager hands.

Adventure's call, we heed with pride,
The flame within, our faithful guide.
In zealous expedition's grace,
We find our purpose, seek our place.

Burning Moments

In the quiet of the night,
A flame ignites within our hearts,
Whispering tales of ancient light,
Where love begins and never parts.

Time cannot dim the fervent glow,
Of passion's fire, bold and bright,
Moments fleeting, yet we know,
Their embers warm our darkest night.

Each kiss, a spark that lights the air,
A dance of shadows intertwined,
In burning moments, we declare,
Our souls forever will be blind.

These memories, a blazing trail,
Through endless hours, fierce and wild,
In every breath, in every wail,
Burning moments, free and unexiled.

Amid the ashes, hope remains,
A testament to what we've shared,
For even as the fire wanes,
Its legacy, undeterred, unpaired.

Spark of Resolve

In the dim light of morning's break,
A spark awakes within our core,
Fanning dreams that never quake,
To strive and conquer, evermore.

Through trials harsh and shadows deep,
Our spirits rise against the storm,
No burden too immense to keep,
Where hearts are fierce, and will is warm.

Each step, a testament to might,
Unyielding to the weight of fears,
In every dawn, renewed with light,
A resolution that perseveres.

We navigate through winding paths,
With courage as our guiding star,
Resolved in purpose, free from wraths,
To reach beyond where limits are.

These sparks ignite a boundless flame,
Of dreams pursued with fervent zeal,
In every pulse, we find and name,
A strength that's true, a force that's real.

Thunderous Hearts

In the hush before the storm,
When all the world is still and calm,
Our hearts ignite, our passion warm,
A silent pulse, a sacred psalm.

The thunder breaks, the skies adrift,
Our spirits rise with tempest's roar,
In every clash, in every rift,
Our love endures, forevermore.

With lightning's flash, our eyes alight,
Illuminating paths unknown,
In storm and sun, through day and night,
Together, never more alone.

The winds may howl, the seas may rage,
Yet arm in arm, we face the fray,
In thunderous hearts, we find our stage,
And dance through life's tempestuous play.

For storms may pass, and skies may clear,
But in our hearts, the echoes ring,
Of thunderous love, sincere and dear,
A bond that time and fate will sing.

Chasing Horizons

Beyond the reach of setting sun,
Where dreams and fears unite,
We chase horizons, one by one,
Guided by their fading light.

Across the fields of endless hope,
Through valleys deep and wide,
With every step, we learn to cope,
With shadows by our side.

We climb where mountains kiss the sky,
And rivers carve their song,
In chasing horizons, we defy,
The doubts that pull us wrong.

The journey long, the road unknown,
Yet onward still we tread,
With each horizon we have grown,
In every tear we've shed.

For at the edge of every dream,
A new horizon calls,
In chasing them, we find the gleam,
Of purpose in our falls.

Burnished Skies

In hues of amber, evening falls,
The horizon burns with fire's calls.
Stars awaken, twilight's kin,
Night's embrace is set to begin.

Upon the canvas, sunset dreams,
A world aglow in golden beams.
Softly sung by zephyr's song,
Where shadows stretch, and nights prolong.

Clouds ignite in crimson waves,
Against the blue, the sun behaves.
The burnt sienna gently fades,
As twilight's lavender invades.

The earth exhales a tired sigh,
As day departs, a soft goodbye.
And in its wake, a silent rise,
The tranquil breath of burnished skies.

Beneath the canopy of night,
The stars alight in silent flight.
In whispers soft, the world complies,
To the serenade of burnished skies.

Ember Trails

Footprints glowing, ember trails,
Whispers of the autumn gales.
Leaves afire in crimson dance,
Nature's fleeting, fierce romance.

Through the wood, the pathways blend,
Where time and seasons intertwine,
Every turn, a story to send,
In fading light, memories align.

Beneath the boughs, gold embers burn,
Each step taken, shadows churn.
Whispers rustle, branches sway,
A journey calls, without delay.

The sky, an amber tapestry,
Embroidered with the leaves that flee.
Through twilight's glow, we traverse,
Upon this glowing, autumn verse.

As night descends, the fire fades,
Into the dark, the ember wades.
Yet in our hearts, the trail remains,
Lit by memories' quiet flames.

Wildly Alive

Through forests dense, the heart beats wild,
In nature's arms, a fervent child.
Whispers of a wild embrace,
Life's raw echoes, nature's grace.

Rivers dance with gleaming light,
Mountains stand in rugged might.
In every breeze, a silent shout,
Of life, untamed, without a doubt.

Leaves fall in a whispered song,
To the earth, where they belong.
Each branch, each root, each living thing,
Part of what this wild brings.

Through valleys deep and skies so high,
Wildly alive, we learn to fly.
Eyes break free from worldly ties,
To nature's call, we rise, we rise.

In every beat of earth's own heart,
We find where wild and life both start.
Together in a dance, we thrive,
Forever, fiercely, wildly alive.

Kindled Realities

In dreams alight, we find the skies,
Where thoughts ignite and shadows rise.
A tapestry of whispered tales,
Kindled by the stardust trails.

Each night we weave our own design,
A blend of truth and altered time.
Reality in ember glows,
Where mind's eye sees and feeling flows.

Beneath the moon's enkindled light,
We craft our worlds from dark to bright.
Ideas soar on wings unfurled,
In this dreamscape, another world.

A spark within the quiet dark,
A flame ignites, a tiny spark.
From shadowed doubts to hopeful gleams,
Kindled realms unfold through dreams.

As dawn approaches, skies reclaim,
The painted dreams, the whispered name.
Yet in our hearts, reality's bound,
To kindled truths our minds have found.

Sultry Ventures

Beneath the moon's seductive glow,
Where whispered winds in darkness flow,
We wander paths obscure, untold,
In quests where passions dare unfold.

The night conceals with velvet shroud,
Desires spoken not aloud,
We tread on dreams so sweet, so bold,
In sultry ventures, truths unfold.

Stars above in fervent dance,
Invoke a spell, a trance-like stance,
In shadows deep, our spirits blend,
On paths where hearts to love transcend.

A fervid touch, a glance so brief,
Encounters fleeting, full of grief,
Yet in the sultry night we chase,
A love that time cannot erase.

Eclipsed by dawn's first tender light,
Our ventures fade in morning's sight,
But memories of the night remain,
In sultry dreams, we live again.

Radiant Resolve

In dawn's embrace, the world awakes,
With hope anew, the spirit takes,
A journey forth with steadfast will,
In radiant resolve, hearts thrill.

Through trials faced and hurdles tall,
We rise again, we never fall,
For in our core, a fire glows,
In every heart, a courage grows.

Each step we take, with purpose clear,
Dispelling shadows, banishing fear,
With light that beams from deep within,
We face the world, our quest begin.

Through darkest storm and fiercest gale,
Our will prevails, we shall not fail,
For in resolve, we find our strength,
And reach beyond our limits' length.

So let the sun of hope arise,
In every heart, a flame that flies,
In radiant resolve, we find,
The path to peace and love, combined.

Resilient Passion

In hearts that beat with ardent fire,
A love that time cannot conspire,
Resilient passion fierce and bold,
Through years and tears, it still unfolds.

With every trial, its fervor grows,
Like rivers deep where courage flows,
No force can quench or dim its light,
In darkest hour, it's our might.

Through storms of life and tempests wild,
This passion stands, untainted, unfiled,
A beacon bright in midnight's reign,
Through sorrows thick, it bears no stain.

In moments tender, fierce, and sweet,
Where hearts in loving rhythm beat,
This bond endures, through joy and pain,
A love unbreakable, untamed.

So let the world with chaos spin,
Our passion's fire remains within,
In love so pure, resilient, strong,
In every heart, it writes its song.

Explorative Heat

Beneath the sun's relentless blaze,
We tread the paths of wildest maze,
In lands unknown, our spirits fleet,
In search of truths, explorative heat.

With every step, new wonders found,
In every breath, new joys abound,
We venture forth with hearts alight,
Embarking on a quest so bright.

Through deserts vast and oceans wide,
In mountains tall, where dreams reside,
We seek the secrets time concealed,
In explorative heat, revealed.

The world unfolds in colors wild,
Unveiling mysteries beguiled,
We grasp the flames of knowledge sweet,
In every trial, a newfound beat.

So let the sun in fervor shine,
On paths unknown, on quests divine,
In explorative heat, we find,
The boundless wonders of the mind.

Effusive Sprint

Through fields, the wind does swiftly glide,
With whispers bold, it takes its stride.
On paths of gold, where dreams collide,
The effusive sprint won't be denied.

It captures hearts in wild embrace,
A dance of speed, as stars give chase.
Beyond the hills, beyond the space,
In endless race, it finds its place.

No chains to bind, no earthly stake,
Just freedom's breath, each dawn to break.
With spirit high, no fear to quake,
The effusive sprint, for life's own sake.

Each step it takes, a story told,
Of courage young and spirits bold.
In sun or rain, through heat and cold,
The tale of sprint will ne'er grow old.

Oh, how it leaps, with grace so fine,
The effusive sprint through heart and mind.
A force of nature, love divine,
To fleeting goals it is aligned.

Prismatic Drive

With colors bright, the dawn ignites,
A prismatic drive, through day and night.
Each hue a dream, a vision's light,
It paints the world in shades of might.

Upon its path, no shadows grow,
Just vibrant trails, where spirits glow.
In every turn, a cosmic flow,
The prismatic drive will always show.

From red to violet, spectrum's grace,
It dances wild, in boundless space.
A journey through the endless chase,
In every shade, it finds its place.

Through prisms clear, it journeys far,
A ray of hope, a guiding star.
No cloud or storm its light can mar,
The prismatic drive, just who we are.

It bends and curves, yet never breaks,
In every pulse, the courage wakes.
A rainbow's arc, a path it stakes,
The prismatic drive, for all hearts' sakes.

Relentless Cheer

From dawn to dusk, a spirit blithe,
The relentless cheer, it comes alive.
In every laugh, in every strive,
It parts the clouds, on wings we thrive.

Through thick and thin, it holds its ground,
In every heart, it can be found.
A melody of joyful sound,
The relentless cheer, forever bound.

No storm can quench its steady flame,
In every soul, it stakes its claim.
With endless hope, it chants its name,
And through the night, it plays its game.

Each step we take, it walks beside,
In darkest times, it still abides.
A faithful friend, a constant guide,
The relentless cheer will never hide.

With every dawn, a new embrace,
It lights our lives, in steady grace.
Through every trial, in every place,
The relentless cheer, our hearts' own pace.

Ardor in Motion

With fervent beat, the heart aligns,
Ardor in motion, through the times.
In every pulse, a world resigns,
To passion's stride and rhythmic rhymes.

Through valleys deep and mountains high,
It sails on dreams, where eagles fly.
In every breath, a whispered sigh,
The ardor moves, beneath the sky.

No chains can hold, no fetters bind,
A soul in quest, a boundless mind.
With love's own force, it seeks to find,
The ardor's path, forever lined.

In ocean's roar and quiet glen,
The ardor dances, through the pen.
In poems old, in hearts of men,
Its motion told, again, again.

It drives the soul to seek, to dare,
In every gaze and hopeful stare.
With ardor's brush, we paint the air,
In motion's rush, our fates declare.

Ignited Journeys

In twilight's hue the path aligns,
With dreams that fuel each step within,
We chase the stars through darkened pines,
Our spirits blaze where hopes begin.

The forest whispers ancient lore,
In every leaf, adventures hide,
Beyond the ridge, unknown shore,
A world unseen, where dreams confide.

Embers cast in morning light,
Forge the trail we dare to tread,
Through valleys carved in endless night,
Our courage blooms where fear has fled.

In shadows deep, the fires spark,
Guiding hearts that yearn to roam,
With every stride, we leave our mark,
Building futures, finding home.

Ignited journeys, bold and true,
Charting courses through the storm,
With flames that linger, ever new,
We shape the world in every form.

Eternal Drive

Beneath the stars our purpose wakes,
In every heart a fire burns strong,
We scale the heights, cross endless lakes,
With faith that drives our journey long.

Through fate's embrace, we rise and fall,
In ceaseless quest for what we crave,
No night too dark, no dream too small,
Our tenacity like ocean wave.

In every dawn, a new reprieve,
With every dusk, a whispered call,
Days unravel, we believe,
In beating hearts, we give our all.

Mountains loom yet hold no fear,
The climb becomes our solemn hymn,
With every step, our goals grow near,
In shadows cast, our lights don't dim.

Eternal drive within us stays,
A constant flame, a reason why,
Through winding paths and endless days,
Our silent vow to never die.

Bold Rhythms

In every pulse, the beat begins,
A cadence fierce, a life renews,
From humble notes, the song within,
A symphony of myriad hues.

Bold rhythms dance through night and day,
Their tempo flows through joy and strife,
They lead our hearts in fervent sway,
The melody that molds our life.

Hands uplifted in the breeze,
We feel the world's resplendent tone,
In every echo, whispers tease,
A harmony that's all our own.

We march to tunes of dreams surreal,
Through fields of gold, through skies of gray,
With every step, our fates we seal,
In time's embrace, we find our way.

Bold rhythms anchor in our soul,
They guide us through the vast unknown,
In every chord, we find our role,
A tune unique, forever grown.

Relentless Fire

In every heart, a spark resides,
A candle's glow in tempest strong,
Through storm and calm, it ever guides,
A flame that carries life along.

Relentless fire, unyielding blaze,
It fuels our dreams with boundless might,
Through darkest nights and brightest days,
It keeps us warm, it grants us sight.

From ashes rise beneath the moon,
A phoenix pure, a spirit whole,
In nature's song, a timeless tune,
This burning drive ignites the soul.

With every breath, it fans our will,
In every tear, it lights the way,
Relentless fire, a voice so still,
Yet speaks of dawn in night's display.

In endless quest, we heed the call,
The blaze within, our guiding sire,
Through rise and fall, we stand tall,
Embracing life's relentless fire.

Fevered Quest

In twilight's grasp we wander far,
Beneath the moon, beneath the star,
With fevered dreams, our hearts ignite,
On nocturnal roads, we'll fight, take flight.

A quest through shadows, silent scream,
The echoes whisper, what does it mean?
Each step we take, each breath we steal,
Reveals the truths we dare not feel.

Against the tide, the night we dare,
With fervent hope, our spirits flare,
In fevered dreams we seek the crest,
The dawn that marks our fevered quest.

Through valleys dark and mountains high,
With piercing gaze, we scan the sky,
A path uncharted, yet pursued,
By dreams and fears, we're both imbued.

The fever's thrall, a searching hand,
A journey traced in shifting sand,
We run, we leap, we never rest,
Forever on this fevered quest.

Intensity Unleashed

A spark ignites with fierce delight,
Where shadows bend to purest light,
Through storm and flame, we rise, we fall,
In fervor's grip, we heed the call.

The tides of time, relentless, swift,
Through chaos' heart, our souls we lift,
Intensity, a fire untamed,
With wild desire, the night's proclaimed.

A dance of stars in fevered blaze,
Across the sky, through veils of haze,
Our spirits soar on wings of fire,
Unleashed, untamed, with hearts afire.

The pulse of life in rhythm's beat,
Our journey bold, complete yet fleet,
In every breath, the essence flows,
Intensity through veins bestows.

Unleashed, our minds entwine the night,
Through endless dreams, in shared delight,
United by a fervent flame,
Together, we become unnamed.

Driven by Heat

In deserts wide where shadows play,
The blazing sun holds sway by day,
We march through sands, a searing beat,
Our hearts alight, we're driven by heat.

With every step, the ground ignites,
Our spirits climb to fevered heights,
In fervent chase, through fire's embrace,
We're driven by this endless race.

Through nights afire, beneath the moon,
Our souls in fiery rhythm's tune,
The path ahead, with passion's light,
We conquer fear, our hearts ignite.

By sun and stars, through heat's demand,
We journey far, a fiery band,
Where flames and dreams in tandem meet,
Our spirits soar, driven by heat.

One heartbeat strong, in searing sun,
Unyielding hearts, our bond begun,
Through scalding sands, our fate we'll greet,
Together, always driven by heat.

Volcano of Dreams

Beneath the earth, where secrets lie,
A molten heart begins to cry,
With every pulse, our dreams ascend,
In lava's flow, our spirits blend.

The mountain rumbles, restless night,
A searing glow, a fervent sight,
From deep within, the pressure builds,
A symphony, where vision's filled.

In eruption's dance, our hopes take flight,
Through plumes of ash, in darkest night,
A paradise of fiery streams,
Emerges forth, a volcano of dreams.

Through fields of flame, where passion breathes,
In molten rivers, fate bequeaths,
We chase the stars, through fiery seams,
We're bound within this volcano of dreams.

The dawn arrives, the ashes clear,
Our waking souls, no longer fear,
In every ember, hope redeems,
We've conquered in our volcano of dreams.

Spirited Pursuit

Beneath the azure skies so wide,
Runs the zephyr, whispers ride,
Mountains tall that pierce the blue,
Hearts of wanderers, born anew.

Endless roads, horizons merge,
Woods that hide the morning's urge,
Rivers etch the paths unknown,
Every step, to self, is shown.

Golden sands and mystic beams,
Laughter in the silent dreams,
Echoes from the canyons deep,
Stories ancient, vigils keep.

Journey's call, a melody,
Nature's hymn, a symphony,
In the dance of night and dawn,
Spirits rise and then move on.

Each heartbeat, a compass true,
Guiding towards vistas new,
For within the quest, we find,
Treasures waiting, unconfined.

Incisive Zeal

Blade of thought, so keen and bright,
Cuts through shadows, births the light,
Fiery will that fuels the mind,
In our passion, truth we find.

Each idea, a spark divine,
Webs of wisdom, threads entwine,
Questions bold, we dare to ask,
In their answers, break the mask.

Faces stern, yet hearts on fire,
Striving higher, reaching higher,
Intellect, our guiding star,
Chasing dreams both near and far.

Reason sharp as morning dew,
Every angle, every view,
Through the prism of our quest,
Gems of knowledge manifest.

In the fervor of our gaze,
Set ablaze, new future's ways,
With incisive zeal we steer,
Crafting worlds, both bright and clear.

Lustrous Milestones

In the hall of time, we tread,
Footprints in the path ahead,
Each milestone, a gleam so bright,
Guiding through the endless night.

Moments etched in golden hue,
Memories, a treasure true,
Every struggle, every fight,
Makes the journey worth the plight.

Crowning peaks we strive to scale,
Winds that tell a hopeful tale,
Of the triumphs deeply sown,
In the seeds of dreams we've grown.

Through the labyrinth, shadows cast,
We emerge, unbound at last,
Milestones shine, a wondrous lore,
Of the lands we've walked before.

Lustrous jewels in time's embrace,
Glimpses of a fleeting grace,
In each step, a story's tone,
Milestones guide us, carving stone.

Unstoppable Yearning

In the heartbeat's quiet hum,
Whispers of desire come,
Like the stars that pierce the night,
Yearning takes its boundless flight.

Eyes that search the distant shore,
Seeking through the evermore,
Echoes of an ancient song,
Toward the future they belong.

Veins of fire, pulsing dreams,
Flow where the horizon gleams,
Restless spirits, bound and free,
Yearning for what yet will be.

Time's embrace, a fleeting touch,
Yet we crave, we need so much,
In the lore of moonlit skies,
Dreams unfold, no compromise.

Unstoppable, this heart's crusade,
Of desires that will not fade,
In the quest to feel, to see,
Yearning's song, our destiny.

Pulse of Ambition

Beneath the sky where dawn breaks free,
Lies the pulse of ambition, eager to see.
Mountains tall, paths unclaimed,
Driven by fire, spirits untamed.

Steps carved in sand, strides unfazed,
Eyes on the prize, endlessly amazed.
Time may challenge, trials collide,
But ambition pulses, deep inside.

Echoes whisper, dreams ignite,
Guiding through the darkest night.
Heartbeats drum, fierce and fast,
In the pulse of ambition, shadows cast.

Dancing Desires

In twilight's glow, two hearts align,
Dancing desires, in rhythm divine.
Bodies twirl, in passion's flame,
Whispering love, calling by name.

Night's soft serenade, moonlit trance,
Guided by stars, lost in the dance.
Eyes meet in a moment so deep,
Desires awaken from silent sleep.

Hands entwine, movements blend,
A timeless embrace, that knows no end.
In every spin, and gentle sway,
Dancing desires, lead the way.

Unyielding Spirit

Beneath the weight of trials vast,
An unyielding spirit stands steadfast.
Through storm and stress, shadows may fall,
But a spirit so strong, overcomes all.

In fields of doubt, where fears grow high,
Unyielding spirit, reaches the sky.
A heart that perseveres, dreams held tight,
Facing the darkness, seeking the light.

With courage bold, and strength so rare,
Navigating life, with limitless flair.
An unyielding spirit, fierce and bright,
Guiding through night, into the light.

Enthusiastic Race

Through fields of green, we chase the dawn,
With every heartbeat, we press on strong,
Our spirits soar, our feet embrace,
The thrill within, the enthusiastic race.

With every step, a story told,
In eager quest, our dreams unfold,
Eyes fixed ahead, we hold our pace,
Bound by passion, in this ardent race.

The wind our guide, the sky our kin,
Determined hearts, we race within,
A journey vast, we now embrace,
Undefined by time, this endless race.

In sync with Earth, in tune with grace,
We chase the sun, this cherished place,
Hands intertwined, souls interlace,
Bound by the thrill, the enthusiastic race.

Through highs and lows, no fears to trace,
United stride, in this we place,
A legacy of strength and base,
Forever bound, in this endless race.

Lust for Movement

In the beat of every heart we find,
A lust for movement, minds unbind,
Steps that lead to paths anew,
With every breath, a world we view.

Through valleys deep, and hills so steep,
Adventure calls, no time to sleep,
In every turn, a story spins,
The quest for more, where life begins.

The dance of fate, the spin of time,
In every rhythm, so sublime,
We move with fervor, grace, and might,
To capture moments, day and night.

With every pulse, with every sway,
In movement's arms, we find our way,
To places unknown, yet dreams defined,
A yearning path, of body and mind.

Embrace the flow, the constant change,
With hearts entwined, we rearrange,
Our spirits free, no longer caged,
In lust for movement, life's stage engaged.

Glowing Ambitions

Beneath the moonlit sky we stand,
With glowing ambitions, dreams unplanned,
In every heart, a fire burns bright,
Guiding us through the darkest night.

With stars as beacons high above,
We chase our passions, fueled by love,
In shadows cast by doubts and fears,
Our glowing ambitions persevere.

Through stormy skies, through trials faced,
We hold our hopes, they are embraced,
With every step and every stride,
Our dreams alight, they are our guide.

Beyond the clouds, where visions soar,
Our glowing ambitions ask for more,
As dawn breaks forth from night's embrace,
We forge ahead, no dreams erased.

In unity, with strength unbowed,
We voice our hopes, we sing aloud,
With glowing ambitions, hearts combined,
A future bright, for all to find.

Boundless Zeal

In every heart, a fervent spark,
A boundless zeal lights up the dark,
With every challenge, we take the lead,
A passion fierce, a burning need.

From depths of sorrow, heights of joy,
This boundless zeal, it we employ,
To carve our paths, to break new ground,
In every beat, our strength is found.

Through waves of doubt, and tides of fear,
Our spirits bold, we persevere,
With every breath, with every thrill,
We chase our dreams, with boundless zeal.

No mountain high, no valley low,
Can dim the light, the fire we show,
With hearts ablaze, with wills of steel,
We journey on, with boundless zeal.

In unity, with voices clear,
We rise above, we hold life dear,
Our dreams unfold, our truths reveal,
The world awaits, our boundless zeal.

Printed in the USA
CPSIA information can be obtained
at www.ICGtesting.com
LVHW050837310724
786879LV00001B/8